MW00990462

POEMS OF PARENTING

POEMS OF PARENTING

LORYN BRANTZ

WILLIAM MORROW
An Imprint of HarperCollins*Publishers*

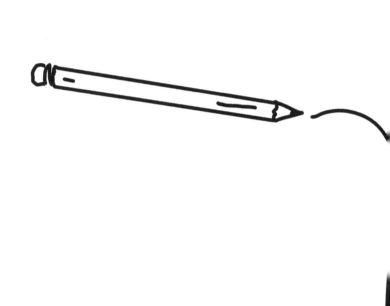

FOR RONEN

Who deprived me
of so much sleep
I lost my mind
and couldn't stop
writing poetry

PART I

Wrinkly Baby Bean

Small and New

You Are Here

OTHERWORLDLY

The moment you were born
They placed you on my chest

Miraculous
Otherworldly
Truly a gift

I looked down
and around
To my partner
My love

and thought
This is by far

The weirdest shit
We have ever done

THIS TALL TO RIDE

I waited and worried
for two pink lines

I waited and worried
for the weeks to go by

I waited and worried
for you to arrive

I waited and worried
to make sure that you thriv

I waited and worried
and waited and worried
and waited until I realized

I'm missing
One heck of a ride

WARM BABY LOAF

When you are born

They call

  Height

    "Length"

'Cause you're just

This laid-out

Little

  Flop

    Peanut

      Body

    Cutie splooty

        Baby

          loaf

WISH

I used to come here
and wish for you

Now we come here together

BARNACLE BABY

Barnacle baby
Won't be put down
Barnacle baby
be carried or frown

Barnacle baby
I know you need me
But Barnacle baby
my back
is
hurting

RUN TO YOU

If you coughed
Five thousand miles away
I would probably hear you
And come running there—

SHE'S GLOWING

I feel
The glow
of Motherhood

Like someone
put wadded hair
In a blender
With sweatpants
And gently poured it out
On the counter

Placed raisins for eyes

The glow
seeps out

Sometimes when I breastfeed
I look down
and think
Wow
This will be a full-grown adult someday

That's really

Really
really weird

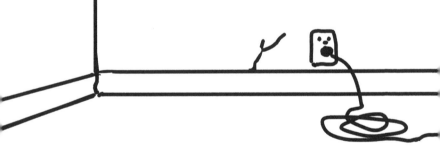

REALLY REALLY REALLY WEIRD

THE MOUNTAIN

Little
by
   little

Step
   by
      step

I will overcome this mountain

And I will look back someday
And think fondly

On this pile
of teeny
tiny
little
clothes

DOUGH BABY

Pop and fresh baby
Straight out of the crib

Warm little body
Plump squishy cheeks
Cashmere cotton hair

If I could package this up
It wouldn't last long
Too delicious to save

Devour it now
Before it's too late

MOM JOY

Almost forty
Finally realize
what my body is for

It's not for you
it's not for them
My children come close, but not even then
It's really for me

To carry my brain
Which holds more than expected
Stroll around Target
Solve big problems
Do nothing

Soft fleshy mush
Watch out everyone
Here comes my tush

My baby is sleeping on me
So precious
The weight of their body
So sweet
so calm

I am fucked

TRAPPED

Like a moth

to a flame

Baby hand

to my cup

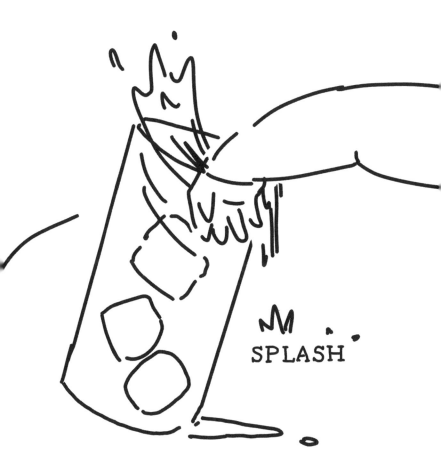

SPLASH

BREATHE

Are they breathing

Are they breathing

Are they breathing

Are they—

Am I breathing?

So you've had a baby
Let me tell you what to do
Teach them this trick before they turn two

It is the most important skill they will learn
They will do it nonstop but it rarely gets old
OK maybe sometimes
But it's still worth its weight in gold

Get out your bottles and cups
Hold them right up
Teach your baby to *Cheers*

At times your arm will get tired
And it's been 100-plus times
But even then it's the best
Awe-inspiring
baby hands
cuteness-fest

Le Fog

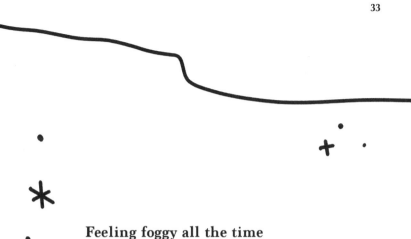

Feeling foggy all the time
But also remembering everything ever
All at once

Need to order more socks before I forget
Being a mom sure is
Something
else

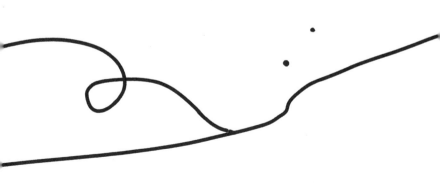

GOOD BABY

I know people say
not to ask
Are they a good baby?
'cause what's that anyway

But I just have to say
you my friend
are one
very
Very
good baby

How is it possible
For me to be so tired
And you so awake

I try not to project my tiredness on you
But don't we both need a nap
Maybe a cuddle for a few?

Turns out it's just me
Exhausted on my back
While you dance around my body
Asking for a snack

HOW

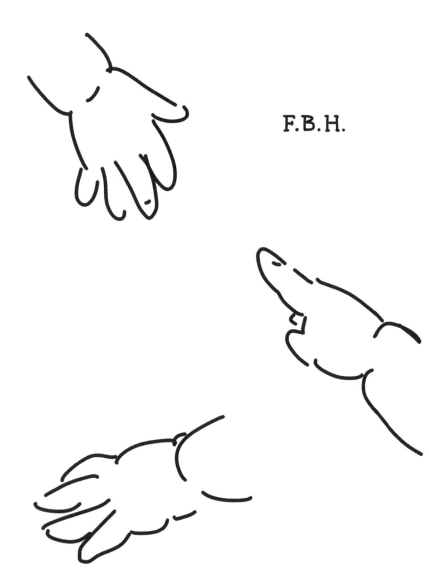

F.B.H.

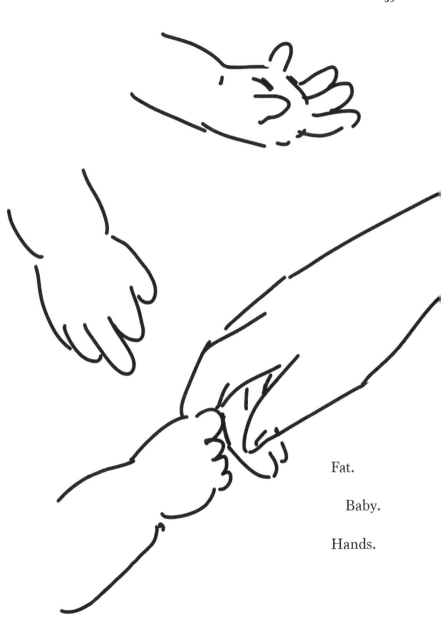

Fat.

Baby.

Hands.

PART II

Squishy Dumpling

On the Move

Welcoming You

To Babyhood

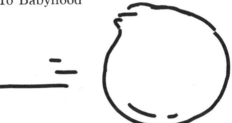

THE LIMITS OF MY MIND

That nose
Those cheeks
and lashes
Small toes

Meeting you
Seeing you
showed me there are limits
of my imagination

because I never
Ever
could have conjured up
In my mind

Someone so
Shockingly
utterly
painfully
Perfect

WARM JAMMIES

I never gave much thought
to what it would be like
If a rabid raccoon
was dipped in oil

And I had to dress it
in a three-piece suit

Until I tried to put
Warm jammies on you

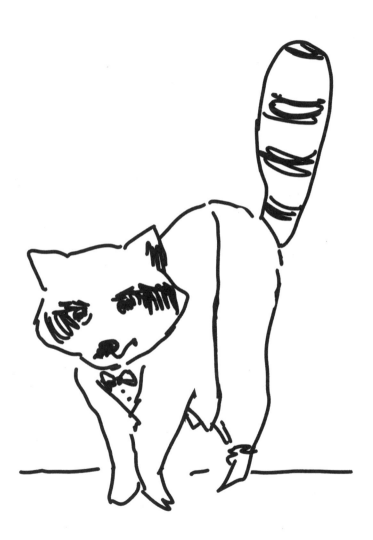

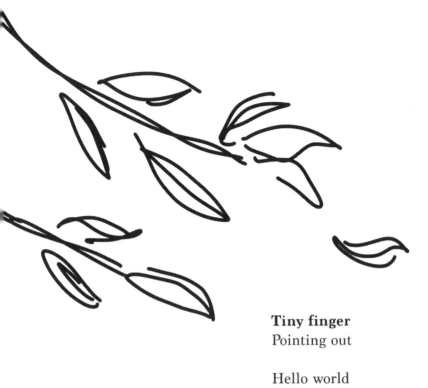

Tiny finger
Pointing out

Hello world
Hello dog
Hello tree

A whole world
Brand-new

Let's sit here
and watch it all
for more than
just a few

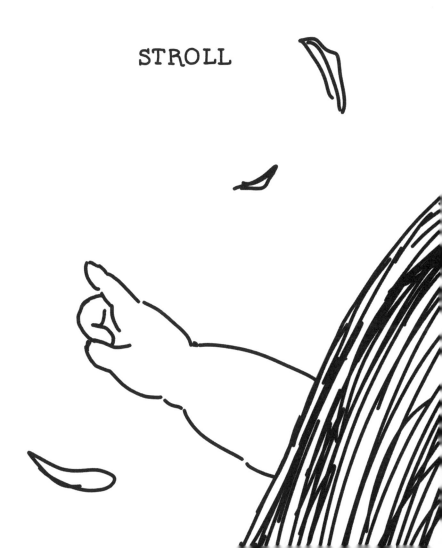

STROLL

48

DELICIOUS

It is the most precious
how you share food with me

Tiny pieces in baby hands
Stretching, look see

Your smile grows wide
Eyes shining with pride

For that expectant sweet face
I'll take a small bite

Warmed from sticky lil hands
Tastes like

        absolute

           shite

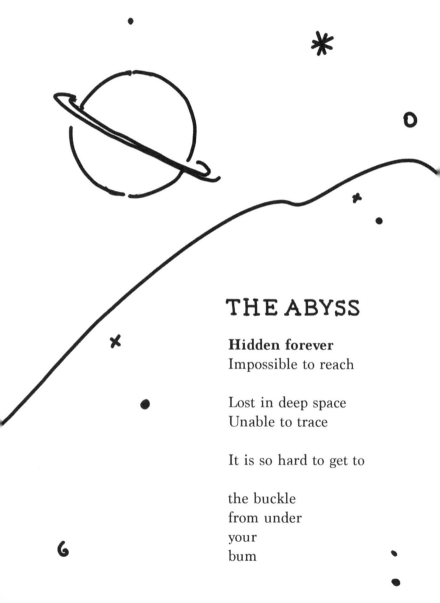

THE ABYSS

Hidden forever
Impossible to reach

Lost in deep space
Unable to trace

It is so hard to get to

the buckle
from under
your
bum

EVERYTHING NEW

Cup
Car
Banana
Bean

Everything new
Never been seen

Door
Spoon
Grass
Tree

Never thought I
Could teach anything

This is a hat
This is a cat

Eventually you'll probably know
more than I do
But for now look there it's a cow
It says moo moooooo!

When I trim my baby's
Sweet tiny nails
Oh so carefully
One by one
Week after week
I can't help but think
Damn
this is
A lot of work

TINY TALONS

ROYAL BABIES

The back of your little head
Strolling down the street
Perfect posture
Little face looking upon your kingdom

I am but your milk maiden
Your dad is a servant
These little babies
Run this town
The cutest tyranny

You are the most beautiful
Gorgeous
Adorable
Human
I have
Ever seen

Coincidentally
You also
Look like
a tiny
me

MY MINI

DINNER PLATE

Night after night
Plate after plate
Grain veggie fruit
Protein in place
Watching it never go
Into the mouth on your face
Trying to be chill and breezy
A healthy relationship with food
Is the mom I'd like to be
Sitting with a smile
Secretly thinking all the while
From a global standpoint

this is super fucked-up

    Oh my God the waste

  The waste

MONITOR

It will be hard for me
To unplug your monitor
If I could watch you at 43

Sitting at your work
Making sure you take lunch breaks
Making sure you're happy

How can I unplug the monitor
When I care so much to see
I promise it's not creepy
I'm just a silly mommy

OK that came out creepy
Please just ignore me

PHOTOS OF YOU

Late at night
I look at photos of my kids
They are so cute
So precious
So pure
I hear a cry in the dark
And I think
Omg shut up I'm trying to look
At photos of you

Banana string
Candy wrapper
Orange peel
Used tissue
Chewed-up chicken
Gum from heel

Pass it on over
It's your mom
Beautiful
Walking human
trash bin

WALKING TRASH BIN

DISCONNECTED

I want to disconnect
I want to be more present

But in my phone lives
my friends
family
my job
Groceries

My clothes
Pediatrician and news
Appointments and shoes
So many photos of you

My connection to the world
Outside this mother bubble

And so
So
many funny
Internet
Jokes

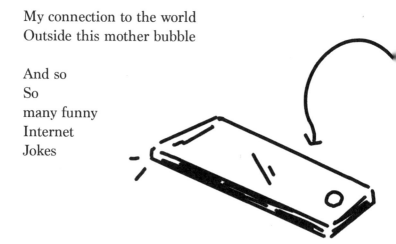

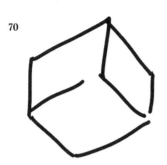

THE LITTLE THINGS

It's hard to describe
How amazing it is
Watching you do little random things
Like taking objects in and out of a bag
With your tiny little hands

It seems kind of silly
But the fact that you're here
And do little random things

Is awe-inspiring to me

Wait don't put that in your mouth
It's a choking hazard

OK back to being in awe
The most amazing little things
I ever did see

Kitchen a mess

Objects everywhere

My kids are asking

Snacks

Everywhere

My husband randomly hugs me

From behind

I don't want to be dramatic

But

I might vomit

and die

OVERSTIMULATED

I order

Again

And again

Again

And again

How could someone so small

Need so many

Bananas

THIS IS BANANAS

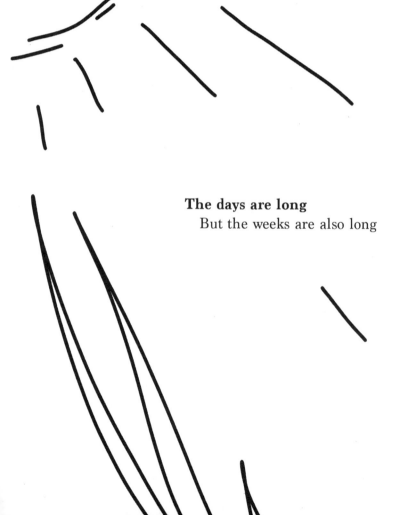

A FEW WORDS TO INSPIRE

The days are long
But the weeks are also long

It's not always easy
But it's always hard

SPROUTS

My little baby
I'm glad
your emotional complexity
Is starting to grow

You are no longer
A small rolling
Potato

But omg
Calm down
It's just an empty paper coffee cup
You want to hold
Give me one second
One last sip
OK
Here you go

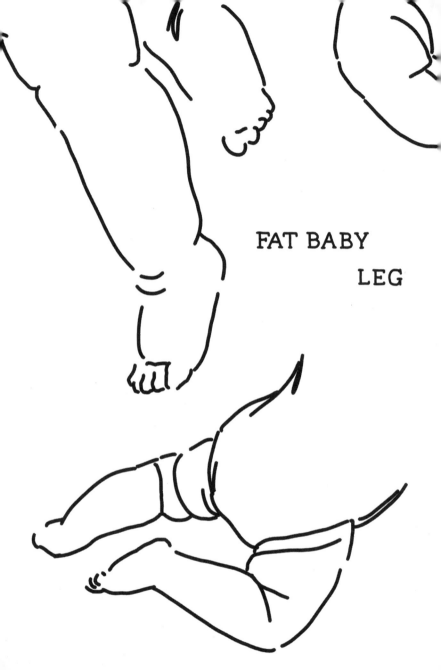

FAT BABY

LEG

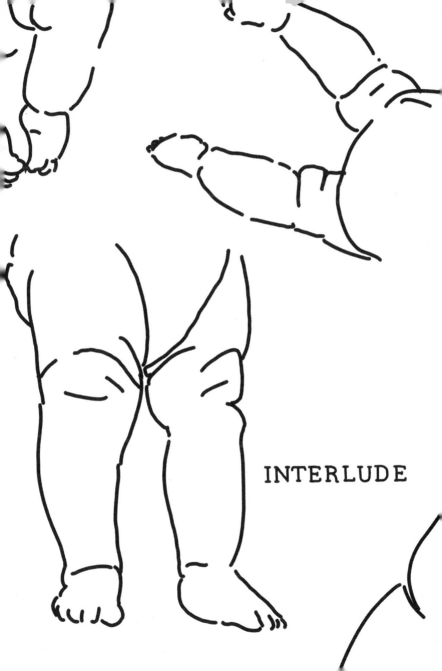

INTERLUDE

PART III

Spicy Little Nugget

Agent of Chaos

Toddlerhood Activated

Let's take the long way home
Stop at everything
What's this? It's a store
What's that? It's a restaurant

Let's take the long way home
How do birds fly? With wings
What's his name? I don't know
that's a stranger
Does he have a dog?
Does he like cats?
Do you think he ever wears funny hats?

It's going to take us a really long time
to get anywhere
We're barely even there
But that's OK
Let's take the long way home

THE LONG WAY HOME

MOM FASHION

Mom fashion

Crocs and socks

Baggy jumper

Hair in knots

No regrets

you still look hot

Mom fashion

Is just fine

Take that picture

aged like wine

If you don't

You will regret

Not having photos

from

this

time

PLEASE

Please

I beg

I know the thought

Is kind

But please

Do not get my child

     another

        Stuffy.

I love my children so much
Sometimes at night
Overwhelmed
I can't sleep

Then they wake early
and I wish
I had slept

fuck.

RISE AND SHINE

8 A.M.

Tea party

Big fight

Hug real snug

Breakfast plate

Play-Doh bake

Silly dance

TV time

Snacks *times* five

Have a cry

Hug some more

Check some phlegm

All of this

Before

8

a.m.

I cannot believe
I created
cell by cell
DNA strands building
In my womb
Miraculously
a new human

Who is now screaming
NO STOP at me
Every time I sing
With this song on the radio
Because I guess
I'm not allowed to duet with Beyoncé
Anymore
or something

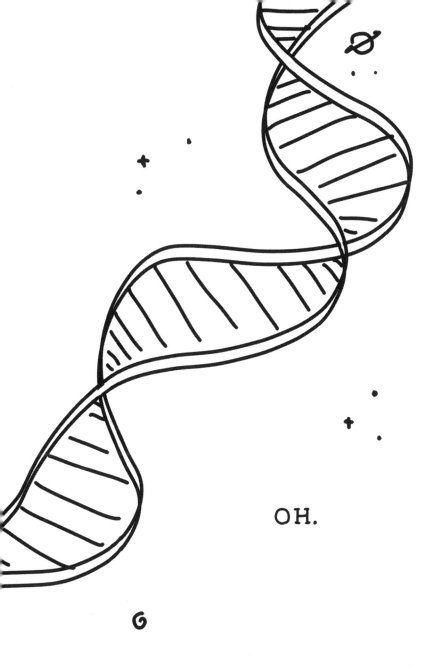

OH.

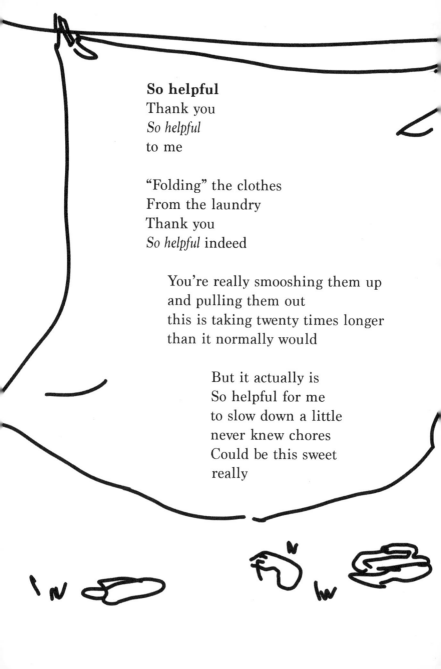

So helpful
Thank you
So helpful
to me

"Folding" the clothes
From the laundry
Thank you
So helpful indeed

You're really smooshing them up
and pulling them out
this is taking twenty times longer
than it normally would

But it actually is
So helpful for me
to slow down a little
never knew chores
Could be this sweet
really

SO HELPFUL

YOUR DAYS

The little photos I get
During the day
featuring you

Excited for
Bits of string
Ripped paper and things

Circle time sitting
Singing and snacks
Dancing
Backpacks

Are the best thing
I've
ever
Ever
seen

99

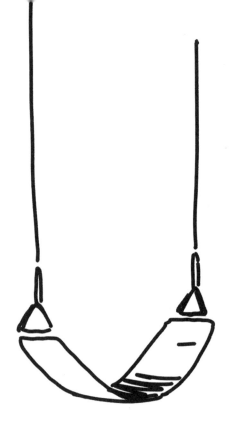

THE ONLY REASON

I held my son
his scream breaking

A tumble from the swings
A little too brazen
A playground miscalculation

The only reason
a child should ever
Bleed

Let's cancel our plans
And put small toys in a line

Let's cancel our plans
And stretch out some slime

Let's cancel our plans
And go to our local bakery

Iced coffee for me
Cake pop for you

Me and my fav
Tiny bestie

TINY BESTIE

Woke up angry
Woke up sad

Only wants mom
Doesn't want dad

Woke up yelling full of rage
I guess this is just the age

Spicy little nugget
Angry mini bean

My tiny raging sweet pea
I'll make sure you feel seen

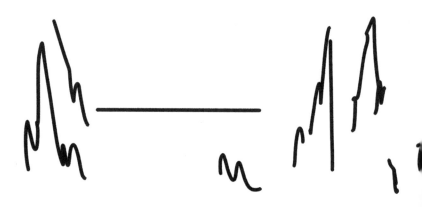

HOW LUCKY

How lucky am I
That we have enough food
You're able to be picky
With what you will and won't eat

How lucky am I
That we have so much
Our place is a mess with toys
Some you don't even play with

How lucky am I
That we have a place to sleep
Even if you won't go to bed
And I'm completely fatigued

How lucky am I
How lucky am I
I can't believe what good fortune we have

We have running water
You still refuse your bath
All things considered
How lucky are we

Becoming a Mother
I wouldn't change a thing
Every step of the way
Every trial
Every win
Every space in between

But I wish
someone had told me
So I could have prepared

Just how much

cleaning

There is

MOTHERHOOD

CODED

ave a snack **Can I have a snack** Can I have a snack Can I have a sna
ave a snack Can I have a snack Can I have a snack Can I have a snac
ave a snack Can I have a snack Can I have a snack Can I have a snac
ave a snack Can I have a snack Can I have a snack Can I have a snac
ave a snack Can I have a snack Can I have a snack Can I have a snac
ave a snack Can I have a snack Can I have a snack Can I have a snac
ave a snack Can I have a snack Can I have a snack Can I have a snac
ave a snack Can I have a snack Can I have a snack Can I have a snac

I have a snack Can I have a snack Can I have a snack Can I hav Can
have a snack Can I have a snack Can I have a snack Can I havCan I
have a snack Can I have a snack Can I have a snack Can I hav Can
have a snack Can I have a snack Can I have a snack Can I havCan I
have a snack Can I have a snack Can I have a snack Can I hav Can
have a snack Can I have a snack Can I have a snack Can I havCan I
have a snack Can I have a snack Can I have a snack Can I hav Can
have a snack Can I have a snack Can I have a snack Can I havCan I

I'm starting to suspect what you really want

is my attention

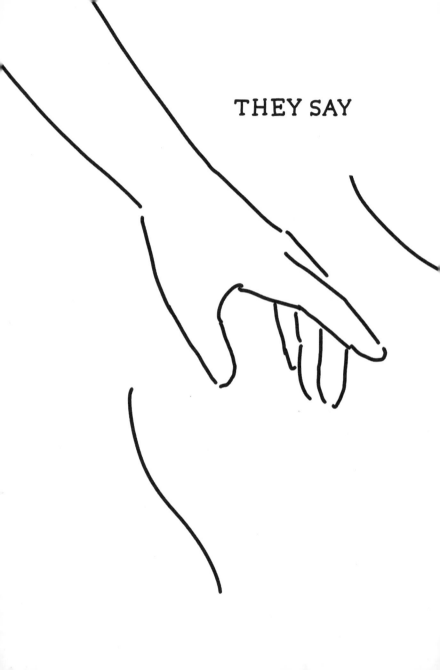

THEY SAY

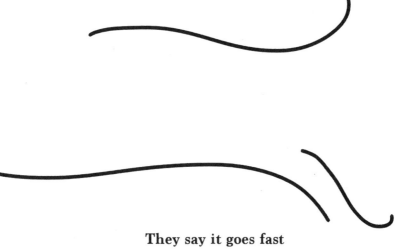

They say it goes fast
So fast
too fast

I didn't believe
Until today
You said to me

Do not hold my hand
and I thought

OH FUCK

SHOES

The most amazing miracle
The most precious to me
My dear one
My life

For the love of God
put on your shoes

So we can go

to the zoo

You may notice
In this poetry
Quite a bit of redundancy
The tired
The awe
Snack time
And awe
Nap and play
Snack listen and say
Parenting is full of redundancy
Repetitivity
Scheduleocity
Day in
And day out
It goes roundabout
You're living
The poetry
Of
Parenting

POETRY OF PARENTING

MOTHER'S DAY EVE

Mother's Day Eve
A lesser-known holiday
Stay up late
scroll all night

Your partner is on morning duty
Good luck to them
Those morning noises you hear
are not
your
problem

MOTHER'S DAY

I never knew
when I served breakfast in bed
what was really going on
in my mother's head

Now I know better
Now that I'm Mom

The crumbly toast
and spilling juice
is actually kind of stressful

But she was still happy
even if it wasn't

really
so
restful

DREAM TEAM

Two weirds fall in love
And have another

Dance party freeze stop
Kick scream crying mad
Won't sleep silly fun
Cuddle puddle on the rug
When all is said and done

Obsessed with this mess
Wouldn't want any other

These fuckers are the best
Dream team family

SAFE PLACE

You come home from school
A long day of keeping it together
It's hard to remember
When you can finally let go
Your tantrums and cries
Are trying to communicate

I'm scared

    I'm angry

       I'm tired

        I'm mad

            I'm here

            I'm here

            I'm here

            I'm here

I know you are here
Loud and clear

I'll be here for you
Do not ever fear

Home is your safe place
Now please
My love
stop hitting me
directly
in
the
face

It's OK to be angry
But it's not OK to hit

It's OK to be angry
But it's not OK to throw

It's OK to be angry
But it's not OK to yell

It's OK to be angry
But it's not OK to buy tickets to Peru
and start a new life
as a park ranger

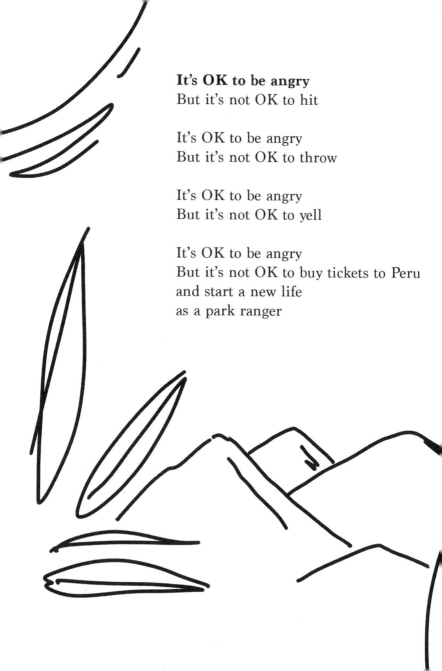

PERU

There is no sweeter sound
than your tiny chipmunk voice

Happy

Playing

Safe

Overheard
from the other room
in the company of
a trusted adult

while I sit

on my phone

OVERHEARD

Need a minute in the bathroom
Hello, Ms. Rachel

Need to do dishes
Hello, Ms. Rachel

Need to cook dinner
Hello, Ms. Rachel

At any given moment a Ms. Rachel song
Plays in my head

And

I

love

it.

Thank God for Ms. Rachel

keep **Keep going** keep going keep going Keep going keep going kee
keep Keep going keep going keep going Keep going keep going keep
keep Keep going keep going keep going Keep going keep going keep
keep Keep going keep going keep going Keep going keep going keep
keep Keep going keep going keep going Keep going keep going keep
keep Keep going keep going keep going Keep going keep going keep
keep Keep going keep going keep going Keep going keep going keep
keep Keep going keep going keep going Keep going keep going keep
keep Keep going keep going keep going Keep going keep going keep
keep Keep going keep going keep going Keep going keep going keep
keep Keep going keep going keep going Keep going keep going keep
keep Keep going keep going keep going Keep going keep going keep
keep Keep going keep going keep going Keep going keep going keep

Keep going keep going keep going Keep going keep going keep goi
Keep going keep going keep going Keep going keep going keep goin
Keep going keep going keep going Keep going keep going keep goin
Keep going keep going keep going Keep going keep going keep goin
Keep going keep going keep going Keep going keep going keep goin
Keep going keep going keep going Keep going keep going keep goin
Keep going keep going keep going Keep going keep going keep goin
Keep going keep going keep going Keep going keep going keep goin
Keep going keep going keep going Keep going keep going keep goin
Keep going keep going keep going Keep going keep going keep goin
Keep going keep going keep going Keep going keep going keep goin
Keep going keep going keep going Keep going keep going keep goin
Keep going keep going keep going Keep going keep going keep goin

It is only two more hours

till bedtime

keep going

THE FINISH LINE

PART IV

Saucy String Bean

Surrender to Parenthood

This Is Your Life Now

PARENTING SCIENCE

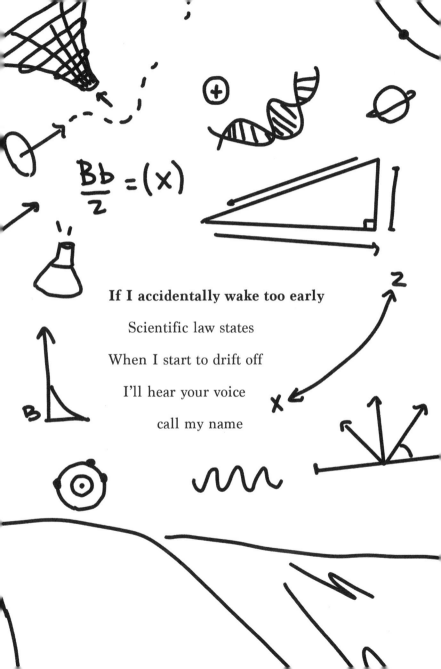

If I accidentally wake too early

Scientific law states

When I start to drift off

I'll hear your voice

call my name

OASIS

I'm writing this poem
from the bathroom

It's the only time
I truly have to myself
My family is probably wondering

Where I am

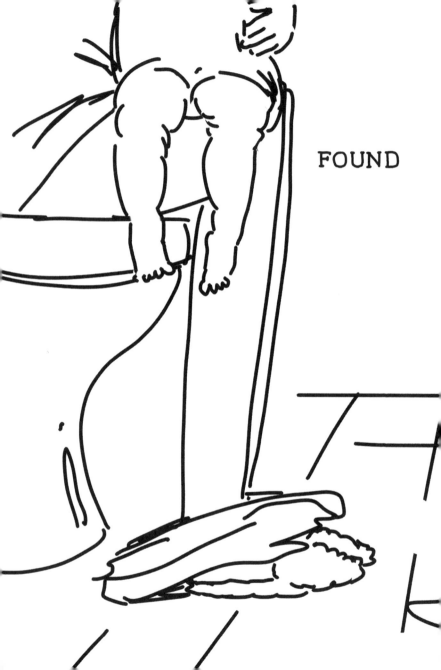

FOUND

You're insisting
on sitting on me
While I go
potty

Apparently
there's no other place
You'd
rather
be

I give up
You can sit here
While you still want to be
So near

Someday if I tell you this
you might think
It is
kind of
weird

Twos twos
"Terrible twos"

What ever are we
going to do!

Can't wait till they're three
Goodness me

Wait

This is

Significantly

Worse

THREENAGER

FATHER'S DAY

I love watching you with our kids
Even just sitting on the couch
End of the day
Sunsetting
Tangerine rays

Holding them near
total absence of fear
On their sweet happy face
As you body slam them
into a soft space

You're more than just Dad
You're
their
safe
place

THE STORM

Life is so full
So busy
So much

Something will have to suffer
And get less attention
And for that
I choose
Clutter

Toys rain down on me
Let's dance in this trash storm
We'll remember dancing best
The background is just a blur
You will forget the messy rest

TINY KICKS

Your tiny kicks
were much sweeter to feel
fluttering inside my belly

Than they are right now
against my face
while I try

      to put on

    your

       shoes

LITTLE TREATS

I tell my child
we can't just eat treats
we can't just eat treats
even when all

I eat

    is

    little

  sweet

    treats

War
Famine
The world is on fire

My daughter is screaming
Because I turned off the TV

How do I explain to her what luck is
How do I explain to myself what luck is

TV TIME

MIRACULOUS

Everything you do
Everything you say
Is the most miraculous
Thing I've ever heard
In every way

Like stars bursting
through skies of black

Even when asking
For your five hundredth

pre-dinner

snack

NIGHT DANCE

We used to stay up all night
So buzzed on new love
Tossing turning
Tangled-up fun

Now we stay up all night
Because our children
Are trying to kill us
By sleep deprivation

We won't let them win
I'm so grateful we're a team
Even when our sanity
Unravels at the seam

WEEKENDS

Do not tell me

You hope

my weekend

is restful

Do not tell me
You hope
I recharge

Tell me
you hope

I survive

YOU ARE FOUR

Total nonsense comes out of your mouth
These stories barely make sense
I am obsessed
With every
fucking word
Of it

You are four.

TIME IS AN ILLUSION

I must confess
Sometimes, I say five more minutes of TV

But your handle on time
isn't so strong

I wait about one
and then
we are done

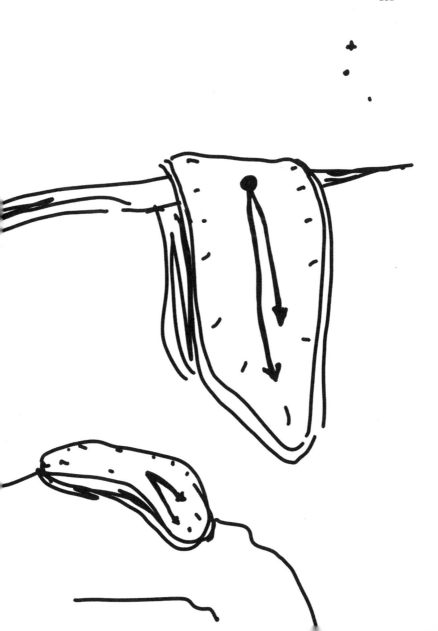

MOM VISION

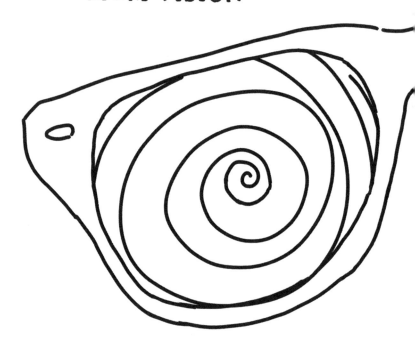

Mom Vision Activate
Choking hazard
Fall risk
Breakable porcelain dish
Unleashed dog
Brain fog

How to refocus
Your Mom Vision
Turn the knobs
On the sides
To not miss good times
From anxiety

brewing

inside

CERTAIN FATE

Getting ready two hours early
To avoid certain fate

Something's missing
a shoe
a toy

Someone's crying
Baby's laughing
found the toy

Other kid decided they'd rather not go

We have small kids
please excuse us
It's our fate
We will
unfortunately

Always

always

Be late

COMEDY

Sometimes you say things like
you smell
like an acorn

And I
am a pinecone

While you talk to your boss
Mickey Mouse
On a fake phone

It must be told
Nothing can prepare you
For the distinct comedy
Of a four-year-old

SCREEN TIME

My daughter wants snacks
And to watch TV

I want snacks
And to watch TV

At what age do I

    just let her

    be

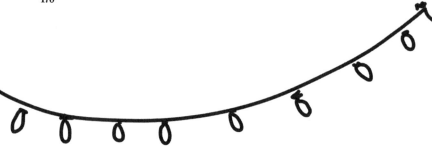

At a family event
Hiding in the guest room

Someone is probably
watching my kids

I hope

HOLIDAY

PRINCESS-SIZED

My five-year-old said
she was getting too big
for her favorite princess dress
She has to squeeze in

I said
You are not meant
to fit to your clothes
Your clothes
are meant
to fit to you

We will go buy

A

Bigger

Dress

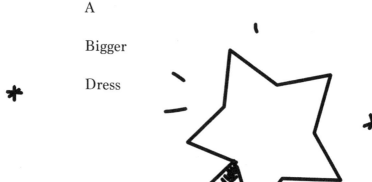

THE WONDERFUL THINGS

The wonderful things you will be
Do not really matter to me

You could make lots of money
Or win a big prize
Get lots of degrees
Learn how to keep bees

Or just sit on the couch
And exist
Healthy happy

So proud of you
no matter what you do

Can't help but think
Why can't I feel this
for myself too

BUBBLY

A little champagne
At the end of each day

Take one of the many berries
You buy for your kids
And plop it right in

A little more fancy
A little more fun

You deserve a little treat
For all that you've done

EPILOGUE

When I leave here
I need you to know
No one has ever loved another human as much

When I leave here
I need you to know
I'm not gone
I've just dispersed quite a bit

When I leave here
I need you to know
I ushered you into this life
With the intent that you enjoy it
With the intent that you live it
With the intent that you see it

For all that it is
For all that it isn't
Never let my absence
Interfere with living fully in it

UNHINGED GRATITUDE

Acknowledgments.
Where do I begin?
The beginning of time
Creative Sublime
I thank The Universe for the chance to be alive
To be in this exact moment
With this exact arrangement of cells
That created me and my family
That feeling that you just can't describe
When you stop for a moment and look inside
and your heart overflows and you don't know why
That we don't have the words for but can feel anytime
in the quiet spaces in between
When you sit and slowly sip tea
if you just stop and watch a rustling tree
Always available for free
and you can't help but just know
There's more to all this
Than just you and me

For the love of my life
My husband
Best friend
Collaborator
After I met you I never doubted anything ever again
My soulmate
True fate
From the very first date
Some of the things we have been through
would bring others to their knees
But we keep on going
Loving so hard you and me

My children, Dalia and Ronen
King and Queen of my heart
Sometimes I can't even tell where I end and you start
If you ever doubt anything ever just come here and read
I want you to see this in print
That you are everything
Your reason for being is just that just to be
A miracle a blessing and everything in between
To live at all is success and you've already achieved
So enjoy every moment
Don't overthink anything

My parents, without you I wouldn't exist
and neither would any of this
Thank you for speaking to me in such a way
That filled my mind with so much kindness
When the world in all its roughness became more clear
My brain stood by me with softness in the face of fear
It's all embedded in me unconsciously
Everything you've ever said and done for me

My agent and editor, Ed and Laura
Ed, your belief in me carries me through
it's unrelenting so strong
Laura, you slid into my DMs at just the right time
I'm so grateful that you wanted this book every line

My neighbors
My friends
My community
Sullivan Street Bakery
For endless delicious coffee
The Hofmans, Jess Gelman, Kate Lydon
Hell's Kitchen
NYC
There's nowhere else
I would rather be

My high school English teachers:
Mr. Shapiro, Ms. Jewel, and Ms. Herndon
Who made me think for a moment each class
My worth was more than my ass
Trying to impress some gangly boys
With low-cut shirts, piles of makeup
It was only in English class
I could really wake up

My village
My team
Teachers, Doctors, therapies
The people in my life
Helping raise my children with me
Day in and day out
I could never write a single word of this without them
no doubt
Pops Brotter, Uncle Jesse, Grandma Debbi, Zaida, Cody,
Maria, Chelsea, Matty, Audrey, All Brotters, Brantzes,
Gilberts, and Jurkowitzes those with us and not, Sobhana
Laguerre, Avery Sumner, Jessica Rodriguez, Bank Street
Family Center, Stephen Gaynor School, NYpeds, Kerri
Cashin, Amy Hirschhorn, Denise Long, I could go on

Artists, friends, and heroes
Some I've been lucky enough to actually know
Brandon Stanton, Rachel and Aron Accurso, Nathan Pyle
Influence me more than they realize
Always trying to do what is right
Staying squarely in the light

From The Universe
To my little place
Bed and bath
Nose on my face
The microbiome in my gut
That helps me process
The smallest walnut
If you zoom in enough
Galaxies inside
Mirroring the expansiveness outside
it's every little thing
So lucky to be here
Thank God for this
For everything pain and bliss
And for you reading this book
My heart sings
I hope parenting
Is meeting you
Deeply
and
Lovingly

HarperCollins books may be purchased for educational,
business, or sales promotional use. For information, please
email the Special Markets Department at
SPsales@harpercollins.com.

FIRST EDITION

Library of Congress Cataloging-in-Publication
Data has been applied for.

ISBN 978-0-06-342643-6

25 26 27 28 29   TC   10 9 8 7 6 5 4 3 2 1